I0348206

Celebrating Maud

A Tribute to L.M. Montgomery

Art & Poetry by
A.C. Blake

BIRDTREE PRESS

Celebrating Maud: A Tribute to L.M. Montgomery

Published by Birdtree Press

Copyright © 2024 by A.C. Blake

First Edition: 2024
(Updated edition, April 2025)

All rights reserved. No part of this book may be reproduced, stored in a retrieval system, or transmitted in any form or by any means—electronic, mechanical, photocopying, recording, or otherwise—without the prior written permission of the publisher, except in the case of brief quotations embodied in critical articles or reviews.

For permissions, inquiries, or additional information, contact:
birdtreepress@gmail.com
For more about her work visit: annecatharineblake.com

This book is available in the following countries: Canada, United States, United Kingdom, Germany, France, Italy, Spain, Japan, Australia, India, Brazil, Mexico, Netherlands, Sweden, Poland, Egypt, Saudi Arabia, United Arab Emirates, and more.

ISBN 978-1-7340854-8-8

Cover Image: L.M. Montgomery at age 22, circa 1895, Cavendish
Photograph: Lucky, L.M. Montgomery's cat, 1935, Norval
Both images used with permission from the L.M. Montgomery Collection Archives and Special Collections, University of Guelph Library.

Editor: Amanda Peters

Library of Congress Control Number: Applied For

Cover design and illustrations by A.C. Blake

*For Maud, who walked in worlds of wonder and
brought them to life.*

Acknowledgments

This project would not have been possible without the invaluable support and resources from various individuals and institutions.

Firstly, I would like to extend my deepest gratitude to the *University of Guelph* and the staff at the *L.M. Montgomery Collection*. Your dedication and assistance in granting access to essential materials made this work a reality.

I also wish to thank *Kate Macdonald Butler* and the *Heirs of L.M. Montgomery Inc.* for their attention to detail and guidance in using L.M. Montgomery's name.

I want to thank my father, Canadian actor *Bud Browning*, who was my first research partner in this journey, which began in 1999.

To my husband, *Ralph Arnold:* Thank you for your unwavering support and patience. Listening to me speak endlessly about Maud, you strengthened me throughout this project.

Finally, my deepest gratitude goes to my editor, *Amanda Peters*. Your keen eye and insights helped shape this work into a piece I take great pride in sharing.

Contents

Introduction— 1

Part 1: Woman Behind the Words—4

    In Her Quiet Light —5
    Maud's Companions—6
    Spectacles—7
    Empowering Women—8
    Scarcity—9
    Simple Pleasures—10
    A Life in Letters—11
    A Kindred Soul—12

Part 2: Maud's Beloved Prince Edward Island—14

    Home (PEI)—15
    Cavendish: Where Land Meets Sea—16
    Silver Bush: A Garden of Inspiration—17
    Lover's Lane: A Path to Enchantment—18
    Island Stories—19
    Freedom in Education—20
    Where Stories Begin—21

Part 3: Whispers of Inspiration—24

    Glimpses of Literary Muses—25
    Louisa May Alcott—26
    Jane Austen—27
    Charlotte Brontë—28
    George Eliot—29
    Charles Dickens—30
    Sir Walter Scott—31
    William Shakespeare—32

William Wordsworth—33
Literary Reflections—34

Part 4: Literary Themes—36

The Gift of Possibilities—37
Imagination and Dreams—38
The Power of Nature—39
Friendship and Community—40
Love and Resilience—41
Growth and Self-Discovery—42
The Eternal Light of Optimism—43
Identity and Belonging—44
The Light She Left Us—46

Part 5: Literary Companions—48

Beloved Characters—49
Anne Shirley—50
Emily Starr—51
Valancy Stirling—52
Marilla Cuthbert—53
Matthew Cuthbert—54
Diana Barry—55
Gilbert Blythe—56
Rachel Lynde—57
Beyond the Page—58

Part 6: From Green Gables to the Globe—60

Anne's Journey Around the World—61
Anne in Japan—62
Anne in the United States—63
Anne in Europe—64
Anne in Australia—65
Anne in Africa—66

Anne's Enduring Legacy—67

Part 7: Light in the Shadows—70

The Writer's Solitude—71
The Struggles of a Woman Writer—72
World War I and Its Impact—74
Enduring Love—76
Quiet Battles—77
The Art of Resilience—79

Part 8: Enduring Light—82

Humor and Resilience—83
Humility and Fame—84
Celebrating Maud—85

Annotated Bibliography—87

Works by L.M. Montgomery—87
Biographical and Studies of L.M. Montgomery—92
Prince Edward Island—93
Ontario—93
Authors and Works That Inspired Maud—94
Additional Sources—95

Author's Biography—97

Introduction

Lucy Maud Montgomery was born on November 30, 1874—150 years ago—and though her books aren't quite that old, her words still feel alive. They've followed me since I was young, both in Canada and the United States. Her books seemed to arrive just when I needed them, like a wise friend who shows up quietly and always on time.

To those closest to her, she was simply Maud. And to many of us, she still is. Her stories were never just stories. Anne Shirley, Emily Starr, and Valancy Stirling weren't only characters—they were friends. They taught us courage and creativity, what it means to be misunderstood, and how to keep believing in beauty. They gave us permission to dream out loud.

Over the years, I've had the honour of contributing to anthologies remembering writers like Walt Whitman, T.S. Eliot, and Sylvia Plath—voices that shaped literature in their own way. But I always hoped there would be a book just for Maud. One that focused on her light, her struggle, her brilliance. Celebrating Maud is that book for me.

This collection of poems and reflections is written from a place of deep gratitude—for her imagination, her honesty, and her enduring influence. She didn't just give us sunlit fields and raspberry cordial. She knew sorrow and struggle, too. And still, she kept writing. That persistence is part of what makes her legacy so powerful—so real.

She once wrote:

> *If I really wanted to pray, I'll tell you what I'd do. I'd go out into a great big field all alone or into the deep, deep woods, and I'd look up into the sky—up—up—up—into that lovely blue sky that looks as if there was no end to its blueness. And then I'd just feel a prayer.*
> —L.M. Montgomery, The Alpine Path, originally published in Everywoman's World, 1917

There's something in that line that says it all. Maud found wonder, even in the hardest moments. She showed us how to keep looking up—to see, to feel, and to keep writing.

The writing throughout this book flows between poetry and reflection, guided by the quiet cadence of prose poetry. Some might call it lyrical nonfiction or poetic meditation. I simply see it as a way to speak from the heart—to hold memory, admiration, and creative spirit in a form that honours Maud's own delicate dance between light and shadow. These pieces are meant to be read slowly, like a walk with an old friend.

Throughout this book, you may notice a tuxedo cat quietly walking between pages and moments. He is inspired by a photograph L.M. Montgomery once took of her beloved cat. Though the photo was too faint to reproduce, I chose to honour its spirit with an illustrated cat—a gentle guide through the text, wandering as Maud's cats once did: curious, comforting, and always nearby.

Whether you've loved her work for years or are just discovering her voice, I hope Celebrating Maud helps you feel a little closer to the woman behind the stories—the one who gave so many of us a home in her words.

Woman Behind the Words

In Her Quiet Light

In stillness
I trace Maud's steps—
her loves, her quiet joys,
the private places
woven into her stories.

Through the lens of her writing
I see the human
behind the celebrated name.

Her cats, her glasses,
her worn journals and her letters—
the small comforts
of a writer's life
and the heartbeats
beneath her words.

Maud's Companions

In Maud's world,
cats were more than companions—
they were her solace.

Lucky, sleek and bold,
roamed the house,
while Daffy, gentle and quiet,
never left her side.

They left paw prints
on her heart,
their purrs and soft steps
woven into her life.

Spectacles

In a time when girls with glasses
were dismissed—
seen as less delicate,
less desirable,

Maud wore hers with quiet grace,
finding beauty
in the crisp edges they revealed.

Through her tales,
Emmeline Harris,
the shy girl with spectacles,
found her voice—

gently reminding us
that clear vision,
both literal and metaphorical,
is a gift, not a flaw.

Empowering Women

With her words,
Maud gave women strength—
grounded in self-worth
and unapologetic in their dreams,
carving paths
where none existed before.

Her message was clear:
Write your own story.
Speak in your own voice.

She opened doors
and left them ajar
for the next generation
to walk through.

Scarcity

When paper was scarce,
Maud wrote on the backs of letters,
old receipts,
any scrap she could find.

Her unwavering dedication—
creativity flourishing
despite the odds.

She showed us that
being a writer isn't about
having the finest paper,
the perfect tools,
or the right setting—
it's about the words themselves,
the stories waiting to be told.

Through her,
I learned that creativity
doesn't wait for perfection—
it makes beauty
out of whatever is at hand.

Simple Pleasures

In her journal entries,
Maud cherished life's little things—
a quiet morning,
a blooming flower,
the hush of rain.

A cup of tea,
the scent of ink on paper,
the calm of a walk
down a shaded lane.

These moments lifted her spirit,
gave her mind a place to rest,
where her creativity quietly grew—
a life woven with wonder,
shaped by the quiet magic
of small joys.

A Life in Letters

Her journals—
a sanctuary where thoughts
wandered freely,
where silence spoke volumes.

They were a refuge,
a place to grow as a writer,
to wrestle with truth
and nurture imagination.

Later, she revisited those pages,
not to erase,
but to choose—
deciding which truths to share
and which to guard,
preserving a piece of herself
for herself.

In that quiet space,
her craft took root,
flourishing gently
in the stillness of her mind.

We, who love her words
and are journal writers ourselves,
understand this need—
to shape our narratives,
to protect what is ours,
and to keep some corners of the heart
only for ourselves.

A Kindred Soul

In her quiet joys
I find a kindred soul—
a woman who thrived
in the moments in between.

I sit with her now,
among the pages of her life—
learning, listening,
hearing the soft sound
of her voice.

The woman behind the words—
a muse, a friend,
a gentle reminder
that the beauty of life
is often found
in its simplest pleasures.

Maud's Beloved Prince Edward Island

Home (PEI)

In the stillness of red roads
and the whisper of sea breezes,
I walk where Maud once wandered—
though only in her words.

Through fields and over shorelines,
I trace her footsteps—
the heartbeat of an island
woven into every page she penned.

It is here,
on this island kissed by the Atlantic,
that I see Maud—
not only as an author,
but as a girl of PEI—
her stories cradled
by the place she called home.

Cavendish: Where Land Meets Sea

Cavendish—
where waves touched rust-red sand,
and sunsets painted the sky
with hues of quiet joy.

It was Maud's sanctuary,
her heart's quiet refuge.
The cliffs, the fields,
the endless blue horizon—
they whispered stories
only she could hear.

Cavendish was more
than a mere setting;
it was where Maud's soul
felt most at home,
the place where her spirit
wandered freely.

Silver Bush: A Garden of Inspiration

At Silver Bush,
Maud found peace.
Among bright blooms
and tall, sheltering trees,
her imagination took root.

This was her haven,
a quiet place where the natural world
fed her spirit
and sparked her dreams.

Lover's Lane: A Path to Enchantment

Lover's Lane—
a quiet path,
lit softly through leaves,
where whispers float on the breeze.

Here, Maud's imagination wandered.
The trees, the winding trails,
the stillness of the woods
gave her a place
for stories to take root,
for dreams to unfold.

To Maud,
Lover's Lane was no ordinary path;
it was a gentle refuge,
a place where magic lived.

Island Stories

On PEI,
storytelling was a way of life.
The island's legends and lore
shaped Maud's imagination,
nourishing her love
for the written word.

From ghostly whispers by the shore
to the quiet magic of daily life,
her books reflected the rich tradition
of stories woven deep
into the island's culture.

Her characters and settings
carried generations of tales—
passed down through the land,
its people,
and its timeless spirit.

Freedom in Education

For Maud,
education was freedom—
a chance to carve her identity
in a world with narrow paths for women.

With her grandmother's strength behind her,
she saved, she sacrificed,
enrolling at Prince of Wales College,
where two years of study
became one,
driven by her fierce determination.

But Maud's journey didn't stop there.
At Dalhousie,
she joined a rare few—
women studying literature
in halls built for men.

In an age when learning was a luxury,
her pursuit was extraordinary.
Her passion lives on
through characters like Anne,
who dreamed and grew
with every book and page—
mirrors of Maud's own quest
to shape her world.

For Maud,
education was never just a degree.
It was a key,
a lantern,
a door to becoming
who she was meant to be.

Where Stories Begin

I walk the red paths
where Maud found her voice,
where waves and fields
and island stories
became her own.

In the wind's quiet whispers,
I still hear her—
a girl of the island,
a woman of the world.

Her words, rooted in this soil,
grew wings and travelled far.

Yet, like tides returning,
her stories flow back
to this small island—
to the heart of PEI,
where they began.

Whispers of Inspiration

Glimpse of Literary Muses

In quiet moments,
I wander through Maud's pages
and meet her muses—
voices that murmur
words of grace,
wisdom and humanity.

This is a tribute,
a homage to those
who spoke to her soul,
guiding her hand
like whispers through trees.

Voices that resonated,
guiding her creativity,
leaving their mark
on her work.

Louisa May Alcott

Alcott's warmth—
the strength of women
navigating challenges with grace—
became kindred to Maud's tales.

*I am not afraid of storms,
for I am learning how to sail my ship.*[1]

Anne reflects
the quiet courage
of Alcott's heroines,
finding hope in the everyday,
and a fierce will to thrive
through hardship.

---

1 Alcott, Louisa May. *Little Women*. Boston: Roberts Brothers, 1868.

Jane Austen

Austen's sharp wit,
her keen eye on love and society,
became Maud's guiding light.

Through Anne and Emily
we feel Austen's charm—
the dance of humor and wisdom,
her insight into women's lives.

There is no charm equal to tenderness of heart. [2]

Both women painted worlds
where love and resilience intertwined,
where quiet strength defied expectations.

Maud may have drawn courage
from Austen's legacy—
a reminder that even in silence,
creativity can thrive,
and stories, told with heart,
can change the world.

---

2 Austen, Jane. *Emma*. London: John Murray, 1816.

Charlotte Brontë

Brontë's wild moors,
her love and longing wrapped in mystery,
stirred Maud's spirit.

I am no bird; and no net ensnares me:
I am a free human being with an independent will.[3]

In Brontë's words,
Maud found a reflection—
a kindred understanding
of passion entwined with pain,
of freedom forged
through resilience.

---

[3] Brontë, Charlotte. *Jane Eyre*. London: Smith, Elder & Co., 1847.

George Eliot

Eliot's depth,
her moral complexity,
offered Maud a path
into the heart of human nature.

*It is never too late to be what you
might have been.*[4]

In Eliot's heroines,
their grappling with society,
Maud found a mirror
of her own exploration
and strength beneath quiet struggles.

---

4   Eliot, George. *Middlemarch*. Edinburgh: William Blackwood and Sons, 1871-72.

Charles Dickens

Dickens' empathy,
his portraits of life's varied faces,
etched themselves into Maud's soul.

*It was the best of times,
it was the worst of times.*[5]

Through his eyes,
she glimpsed a world—
not just as it was,
but as it could be.

On her small island,
in a Canada still finding its voice,
Maud sought to do for her home
what Dickens had done for his—
to weave the struggles and joys
of ordinary lives
into stories that would endure.

Her words became windows,
her pen a lantern,
illuminating the quiet beauty
of a place often overlooked,
its people no longer forgotten.

---

5   Dickens, Charles. *A Tale of Two Cities*. London: Chapman & Hall, 1859.

Sir Walter Scott

Scott's tales of knights and valor
sparked Maud's imagination,
his love for Scotland touching her own.

O Caledonia! Stern and wild,
Meet nurse for a poetic child! [6]

In his words, she felt the pull of heritage—
a shared reverence for tradition,
for landscapes steeped in untold histories,
and roots that ran deep,
connecting her to her Scottish blood.

---

6   Scott, Sir Walter. *The Lay of the Last Minstrel.* Edinburgh: James Ballantyne, 1805.

William Shakespeare

Shakespeare's words,
grand and timeless,
found their way into Maud's heart.

All the world's a stage,
And all the men and women merely players.[7]

His tales of love,
his wisdom steeped in poetry,
inspired her—
a quiet playwright of her own world,
weaving stories in the stillness of her room.

---

7   Shakespeare, William. *As You Like It.* London: Edward Blount and William Jaggard, 1623.

William Wordsworth

Wordsworth's nature—
its hills, lakes, and quiet paths—
became Maud's refuge.

I wandered lonely as a cloud
That floats on high o'er vales and hills.[8]

Through him
she learned to see the world afresh,
to let the wild places
speak their truths,
and to find peace
in nature's gentle rhythms.

---

8   Wordsworth, William. *Poems in Two Volumes*. London: Longman, Hurst, Rees, Orme, and Brown, 1807.

Literary Reflections

In Maud's work,
a light shines clear—
inspired by those she deeply admired.
From Austen's strength
to Wordsworth's reverence for nature,
their influence flows deep.

Dear old world, she murmured,
*you are very lovely, and I am glad to
be alive in you.*[9]

And in that quiet affirmation,
Maud's muses live on—
woven gently
through all she created.

---

[9] Montgomery, L. M. *Anne of Green Gables,* Boston: L.C. Page & Co., 1908.

Literary Themes

The Gift of Possibility

Through Maud's words,
I glimpse the dreams that carried her,
the quiet hope that spilled
from her pen, shaping her work.

Her imagination soared,
blazing new trails for those
brave enough to follow.

*In this world, you've just got to hope for the best
and prepare for the worst and take whatever God sends.*[10]

In Anne's eyes, I find wonder;
in Emily's heart, quiet courage.

Maud's treasure to us all
wasn't just stories—
it was a way to see the world
in vibrant hues of possibility.

---

10   Montgomery, L. M. *Anne of Avonlea.* Boston: L.C. Page & Co., 1909.

Imagination and Dreams

Imagination—
Maud's gift to the world,
a light that guided her hand
and brought her stories to life.
Her characters dreamed with open eyes,
their hearts filled with wonder.

Anne, with her boundless imagination,
found beauty in the smallest things—
the light on trees,
the whisper of the wind.

She painted her world
in shades of magic,
finding joy
even in the shadows.

Emily, too,
dreamed of distant worlds—
a mind reaching for stars,
yet rooted in the soil of New Moon.

Through these visions,
Maud reminded us
that dreams are not meant to be hidden;
they are the seeds
of who we can become.

The Power of Nature

For Maud, nature was more
than a setting.
It was her sanctuary,
a living force that shaped
the lives of her characters.

In fields and forests,
along the red roads of PEI,
she found her inspiration.

Her journals brimmed
with the rustling of leaves,
the changing seasons,
and the quiet beauty
of the natural world.

Through Anne's wonder
and Emily's bond with the land,
nature became both a refuge
its rhythm a gentle balm
that healed and inspired.

Friendship and Community

In Maud's world, friendship
meant more than companionship—
it was a lifeline.

Anne and Diana,
Emily and Ilse—
kindred spirits,
friends bound beyond words.

Through laughter, shared adventures,
and steadfast loyalty,
Maud celebrated the beauty of friendship,
a force that carried her characters
through trials and triumphs.

Community, too, was essential.
Avonlea, with its nosy neighbours
and deep roots,
mirrored Maud's own home.

The sense of belonging,
of shared history,
was woven into each interaction.

Through character's eyes,
we see the power of friendship
and the comfort of community—
a reminder that even in solitude,
we are never truly alone.

Love and Resilience

Love, for Maud,
was a force of resilience.
It wasn't easy,
it wasn't always kind,
but it was strong,
enduring.

Anne's love for Green Gables,
for Marilla and Matthew,
was born of hardship,
but it flourished—
a quiet love that deepened
over time.

Emily's love for New Moon,
for her family,
was tied to her sense of place,
her need to belong.

Maud, too,
knew the weight of love,
the pain of loss.
But through it all
she wrote of hope—
of love's ability to heal,
to endure.

Growth and Self-Discovery

Maud's characters grew
with each page.
Anne, from a dreamy orphan
to a woman of strength and purpose,
found herself in the fields of Green Gables.

Emily, with her fierce determination,
discovered her voice,
her place in the world.

For Maud,
growth was not a straight path,
but a winding journey—
one marked by doubt,
by discovery,
and guided by an inner sense
of who we are striving to become.

Her stories remind us
that becoming is a lifelong process,
that we continue to discover ourselves
and grow
with each step we take.

The Eternal Light of Optimism

Maud's characters
held onto hope,
even when the world
seemed bleak.

Anne's optimism,
her belief in tomorrow,
was a light that guided her—
a flame that never dimmed.

Emily's dreams,
her visions of a brighter future,
were beacons
in the darkest times.

For Maud,
optimism wasn't about ignoring
the hardships of life,
but about finding beauty
and possibility
in every moment.

Her stories remind us
that even when life is hard,
there is always light to be found—
her legacy of hope
continues to inspire.

Identity and Belonging

For Maud,
home was a fragile dream—
lost with her mother's death,
left behind when her father
built a new life elsewhere.

Raised by grandparents,
she knew how tenuous
the idea of home could be—
its security resting
in the hands of others.

In her stories,
home became more than a place.
It was identity.

Anne wasn't just Anne Shirley;
she was Anne of Green Gables,
her heart anchored
to the red roads and whispering trees,
to the love that made it hers.

As a child,
my family moved endlessly,
back and forth between Canada and the U.S.,
my father's work setting the course.
I often didn't know where we were,
but through Maud's pages,
I found a sense of belonging.

I wonder how many other children,
lost in their own transitions,
have read her words
and felt the same—
that home is where love grows,
where roots take hold,
even in the shifting soil
of uncertainty.

Through Maud,
I learned that home is not just a place—
it is a part of us,
etched into the dreams we carry
and the people who make us whole.

The Light She Left Us

In her words
I find strength,
in her stories
I find hope.

Maud knew the world's shadows,
but she chose to light the way—
with imagination,
with dreams,
with love that healed.

Through her characters,
I see the journey of resilience,
the power of nature's touch,
the joy of friendship,
and the steady light
of optimism,
guiding us all
to believe in the beauty
of tomorrow.

Literary Companions

Beloved Characters

To me—and to us as readers—
Maud's characters were not imaginary.
They were real,
they were friends.

Anne, with her big imagination;
Emily, with her quiet resolve;
Marilla, with her steady strength—
they're more than names on a page.

These characters feel like family,
each carrying a bit of Maud—
the people she cherished,
the places that shaped her,
and the dreams she held close.

ANNE SHIRLEY

Anne,
with her fiery red hair
and boundless imagination,
was more than a character.

She was Maud's hope,
her longing for beauty and love,
and her defiance against loneliness.

*Isn't it nice to think that tomorrow is a new day
with no mistakes in it yet?* [11]

In Anne's optimism,
Maud found her own light —
a reminder that dreams
could transform the emptiest spaces.

---

[11] Montgomery, L.M. *Anne of Green Gables.* Boston: L.C. Page & Co., 1908, Chapter 21.

Emily Starr

Emily,
a kindred spirit
born of Maud's own heartache
and dreams.

She walked the line
between reality and magic,
a soul always reaching
for the unseen world.

Like Maud,
she knew the pull
of untold stories,
of quiet mysteries
waiting to be uncovered.

Valancy Stirling

Valancy, with quiet courage,
stepped beyond the grey walls
of duty and expectation.

In the Blue Castle,
she found her voice,
her laughter, herself.

She taught us that even in silence,
a heart can roar to life—
that love, freedom,
and joy are worth every leap.

Through Valancy,
Maud showed us the hope
that it's never too late
to seek the light
waiting just beyond the shadows.

Marilla Cuthbert

Marilla—
stern but tender—
was inspired by the women
who raised Maud,
women whose resilience and strength
carried across generations,
whose love was steady,
often spoken through actions,
not words.

*I love you as dear as if you were
my own flesh and blood.
And you've been my joy and
comfort ever since you came
to Green Gables.*[12]

Marilla's quiet warmth
was Maud's tribute
to the women
who shaped her life.

---

12 Montgomery, L. M. *Anne of Green Gables*. Boston: L.C. Page & Co., 1908., Chapter 35.

Matthew Cuthbert

Matthew,
quiet and gentle,
a man who spoke love
through silence.

Inspired by the men
who showed affection
in simple gestures.

*Well now, I'd rather have you
than a dozen boys, Anne.*[13]

His heart,
a steady force—
a comfort to those he cherished.

---

13   Montgomery, L. M. *Anne of Green Gables.* Boston: L.C. Page & Co., 1908., Chapter 36.

Diana Barry

Diana,
a friend of the heart,
was Maud's reflection
of true friendship.

*Kindred spirits are not so scarce
as I used to think.*[14]

She was a confidante,
a steady companion,
always ready to stand beside Anne
through the ups and downs
of life's journey.

Through Diana,
Maud celebrated the kind of friendship
that weathers every storm.

---

14   Montgomery, L. M. *Anne of Green Gables*. Boston: L.C. Page & Co., 1908., Chapter 19.

Gilbert Blythe

Gilbert,
a blend of teasing and tenderness,
was more than just Anne's rival.

He was Maud's way
of exploring love—
patient, enduring,
growing from youthful rivalry
into something deeper.

*I have loved you ever since that day
you broke your slate over my head.*[15]

Through Gilbert,
Maud showed us
that love, at its best,
is both kind and constant.

---

15   Montgomery, L.M. *Anne of the Island.* Boston: L.C. Page & Co., 1915.

Rachel Lynde

Rachel Lynde,
with her forthright opinions
and no-nonsense wisdom—
a reflection of strong-willed women.

She spoke the truths
others wouldn't dare to say,
but behind her sharp words
was a heart that cared deeply
for her community.

Mrs. Rachel Lynde was one of those capable creatures who can manage their own concerns and those of other folks into the bargain.[16]

In Rachel, Maud gave voice
to those women
whose strength often went unnoticed.

---

16 Montgomery, L.M. *Anne of Green Gables*. Boston: L.C. Page & Co., 1908, Chapter 1.

Beyond the Page

They live beyond the pages—
Anne with her dreams,
Emily with her fire,
Valancy with her courage,
each woven from Maud's heartstrings.

Each character, a reflection
of the strength, the wonder,
the quiet rebellion she carried within.

Through them
we see the world not as it is,
but as it could be—
full of laughter,
full of love,
full of hope in small,
ordinary moments.

In their flaws
we find our own;
in their triumphs
we find the power to rise.

As they move through time,
their voices carry Maud's spirit—
a reminder that fiction,
at its heart,
is truth dressed
in the colours of imagination.

From Green Gables to the Globe

Anne's Journey Around the World

From the quiet lanes of Green Gables,
Anne's story began
and spread across oceans.

From continent to continent,
her spirit touched readers
in far-off lands.
She crossed borders,
her red braids and lively imagination
becoming symbols of resilience,
of hope,
of dreams unyielding to hardship.

Anne in Japan

In Japan, Anne became *Akage no An*—
'Red-Haired Anne'.

Through Hanako Muraoka's translation,
Anne's voice resonated with post-war Japan.
Her longing for belonging
and resilient heart
spoke to young women
searching for their own place in the world.

*It's been my experience that you can nearly always
enjoy things if you make up your mind firmly that you will.*[17]

Her freckled face, her fiery hair,
became a cultural icon,
symbols of courage, individuality,
and a quiet revolution of hope.

Today, Anne's legacy thrives in Japan—
from manga adaptations to theme parks,
her story transcends time,
a reminder that kindred spirits
know no borders.

---

17 Montgomery, L. M. *Anne of Green Gables*. Boston: L.C. Page & Co., 1908, Chapter 7.

Anne in the United States

Across the vast American landscape,
from small towns to bustling cities,
Anne's adventures took root
in the hearts of readers young and old.

Her fiery spirit mirrored the nation's own—
resilience, independence,
and the belief that dreams are worth fighting for.

*I don't want sunbursts and marble halls.
I want YOU!* [18]

Her fierce heart reflected
the American ideals
of self-reliance
and the refusal to accept limits
on what life could be.

---

18 Montgomery, L. M. *Anne of Green Gables*. Boston: L.C. Page & Co., 1908, Chapter 34.

Anne in Europe

Across the seas,
Anne's story crossed into Europe—
In England, her love for nature,
in France, her fierce independence,
in Germany, her resilience—
each part of her found a home
in hearts shaped by their own struggles.

I'm so glad I live in a world
where there are Octobers.[19]

Though rooted in a small Canadian village,
her story reached far beyond,
finding their way into the lives
of readers across the continent.

---

19 Montgomery, L. M. *Anne of Green Gables*. Boston: L.C. Page & Co., 1908, Chapter 16.

Anne in Australia

Under the wide Australian sky,
Anne's story flourished.

Her optimism mirrored the pioneering spirit
of a nation building itself anew—
her resilience a reflection of those
who carved out lives
in wild, untamed lands.

It's delightful when your imaginations come true, isn't it? [20]

From the outback to the cities,
Anne's journey resonated with the search for identity
in a place that embraced both British roots
and its own rugged, unique character.

---

20 Montgomery, L. M. *Anne of Green Gables*. Boston: L.C. Page & Co., 1908, Chapter 28.

Anne in Africa

In Africa
Anne's story reached across cultures.
Her quest for acceptance,
her dreams of a better life,
resonated deeply
with those navigating the complexities
of identity,
of belonging.

Isn't it wonderful that every day can be an adventure? [21]

Anne's resilience,
though born on Prince Edward Island,
became a symbol of hope—
her courage
a reflection of those
who dared to dream
of brighter tomorrows.

---

21 Montgomery, L. M. *Anne of Green Gables*. Boston: L.C. Page & Co., 1908, Chapter 9.

Anne's Enduring Legacy

Anne's story keeps travelling—
crossing oceans,
touching hearts.

From Japan to America,
Europe to Australia, and Africa—
her legacy endures.

Through adaptations,
television series, stage plays,
and countless translations,
Anne's world lives on.

There is more scope for imagination.[22]

Through Anne, Maud built bridges
between nations and generations—
a legacy of hope,
of love,
of dreams that never fade.

---

22   Montgomery, L. M. *Anne of Green Gables*. Boston: L.C. Page & Co., 1908, Chapter 2.

Light in the Shadows

The Writer's Solitude

Maud's words were her light—
a flame she carried through shadowed times.

In the quiet hours,
she faced unseen battles,
and though the world whispered, "Stop,"
she wrote on—
weaving struggle into story,
pain into perseverance.

Hers was a life not only of success,
but of resilience—
refusing to let the weight of the world
extinguish the spark of creativity
burning within.

The Struggles of a Woman Writer

In a world that demanded women be silent—
Canada, early 1900s,
a time when their voices
were confined to hearth and home—
Maud dared to dream beyond.

Few rights,
fewer opportunities,
yet she claimed her place as a storyteller,
her words breaking through barriers
that sought to hold her back.

But her path was far from easy.

Men ruled the publishing world,
and her talent was exploited.
Her publisher, L.C. Page,
took more than his share,
profiting unjustly
from Anne of Green Gables.

The fight to reclaim her rights
was long and grueling—
legal battles that drained her spirit,
financial burdens that weighed her down.

Yet Maud refused to surrender.
Her resilience, her unyielding will
to protect the integrity of her words,
became its own kind of victory—
a triumph of a woman's voice
in a world determined to quiet her.

Even as she fought against injustice,
Maud continued to write—
her stories became a source of strength,
not only for her readers,
but for herself.

World War I and its Impact

The outbreak of war
cast a long shadow over Maud's life,
bringing with it a sorrow
too heavy to ignore.

She watched as young men—
both near and far—
were claimed by the conflict,
their lives swept away
like leaves in a storm.

At home, like so many women,
Maud bore the weight of war—
the fear, the loss,
the endless waiting.

Her son Chester, still a child,
grew up under the shadow of its violence,
a shadow that loomed
over her family.

In Rilla of Ingleside,
the final chapter of Anne's world,
this weight is keenly felt.
Through Rilla's eyes,
Maud wove her own grief—
her fears for the future—
into a story of coming-of-age in wartime.

The war took much from her,
but it also deepened the threads
of resilience, hope, and survival
that had always run through her work,
transforming loss into stories
that would endure.

Enduring Love

Maud's life was filled with love and loss.
She wrote of deep connections—
bonds with family and friends,
and the pain of losing them.

Her husband's struggles,
her own health issues,
the deaths of loved ones
left her with a heavy heart.

Yet she never stopped believing
in love's power to heal,
even when it came with grief.
Her stories reflect this truth.

Anne's love for Green Gables,
Emily's love for her family,
the enduring relationships
that gave Maud's characters
the strength to persevere,
teaching us that love remains,
even in loss.

Through Maud's words,
I see her journey—
a life woven with joy and sorrow,
with love and loss,
an understanding that both
are essential to being human.

Quiet Battles

Maud knew well the battles within—
anxiety clung to her,
and depression weighed heavy.

In a time when sensitivity
was often dismissed,
and mental health was poorly understood,
she carried burdens too great
for one heart to bear.

Her husband's struggles mirrored her own,
compounding the weight of isolation,
the grief of losing a child,
the unrelenting demands of life.

Treatments existed,
but they were crude and incomplete,
guided by what doctors believed was best.
I wonder:
if her delicate nature,
her anxieties, her creative mind,
had been met with the understanding we know today,
might her path have been gentler?

And yet, even in her darkest hours,
her creativity survived.
Writing became her sanctuary,
a place to transform pain into story,
to light the shadows
with the glow of her imagination.

Her strength was quiet,
her courage steadfast,
leaving us not only stories,
but a reminder—
even amidst the deepest struggles,
the heart can create beauty.

The Art of Resilience

Maud's life was never easy—
marked by hardship,
by silent battles,
and by the unrelenting drive to create,
even as the weight of the world
pressed heavy on her heart.

Yet she never gave up.
Her words flowed
even when her strength faltered,
her imagination soared
even when her spirit felt confined.

Her stories endure,
not only for their beauty,
but for the truths they hold—
reflections of her heart,
her resilience,
her belief that even in the darkest times,
light can be found if we keep moving forward.

In Maud's journey,
I see my own.
As an empathic artist,
I feel the weight of the world's cruelty—
its harshness resting in my body,
a physical ache born of deep sensitivity.
Yet, like Maud, I've learned to carry it,
to transform it into something lasting,
a way to create beauty
even from pain.

Her story reminds me
that through struggle,
we find strength,
and that our sensitivity—
the very thing that leaves us open to pain—
is also what gives us the power
to create light for others to follow.

Enduring Light

Humor and Wit

Maud's humor,
sharp and full of charm,
was a reflection of her quiet strength.

She shared her wit—
a gift that brought her characters to life,
their humor a balm for readers
seeking both solace and delight.

In Maud's world,
laughter wasn't an escape,
but a way to face life with courage,
reminding us that a clever heart
can illuminate even the hardest days.

Humility and Fame

Despite her fame,
Maud stayed humble,
often questioning her worth,
wondering if her words would endure.

In her journals,
she wrote of success as fleeting,
never taking for granted
the love her readers gave.

Her humility is woven into her legacy.
She didn't seek fame,
but simply wanted to tell stories
that would bring joy and comfort.

In doing so,
she created a body of work
that continues to touch generations.

Celebrating Maud

In her words,
I find a mirror—
reflecting not just joy,
but the struggles
and quiet resilience
woven into her voice.

As a child, her characters guided me—
to seek knowledge,
to stand tall in who I was,
to wear my glasses with pride.

As a young woman,
I drew courage from her strength—
to persist,
to carve my own path
through life's unyielding storms.

Maud's stories are more than fiction—
they carry whispers of hope,
casting light into the shadows,
illuminating the darkest corners.

Her legacy lives not in her fame,
but in the hearts she's healed,
the souls she's inspired,
the reminder she's given us all—
that we can be strong yet gentle,
resilient yet tender.

Through Maud,
I learned to write,
to dream,
to trust that no matter what life brings,
there is always hope.

And in her words,
I find gratitude—
for the light she shared,
for the path she opened,
for the stories that will forever guide us home.

Lucky, L. M. Montgomery's cat, Norval, 1935. Courtesy of the L.M. Montgomery Collection, Archives and Special Collections, University of Guelph Library.

Annotated Bibliography

Books by L.M. Montgomery

Montgomery, L.M. *Anne of Green Gables.* Boston: L.C. Page & Co., 1908. This novel introduces Anne Shirley, an imaginative orphan who transforms the lives of those in the fictional town of Avonlea Montgomery's vivid storytelling and character development have made this work a timeless classic in children's literature.

Montgomery, L.M. *Anne of Avonlea.* Boston: L.C. Page & Co., 1909. Continuing Anne's journey, this sequel follows her experiences as a school teacher in Avonlea. The narrative explores themes of growth, community, and the challenges of young adulthood.

Montgomery, L.M. *Kilmeny of the Orchard.* Boston: L.C. Page & Co., 1910. A standalone novel that tells the romantic tale of a young man who falls in love with a mute girl with an extraordinary musical talent.

Montgomery, L.M. *The Story Girl.* Boston: L.C. Page & Co., 1911. This novel introduces Sara Stanley, a captivating storyteller whose tales enchant her cousins and their friends in rural Prince Edward Island.

Montgomery, L.M. *Chronicles of Avonlea.* Boston: L.C. Page & Co., 1912. A collection of short stories set in the fictional town of Avonlea, featuring familiar characters and exploring the lives and relationships of the community.

Montgomery, L.M. *Anne of the Island.* Boston: L.C. Page & Co., 1915. Anne pursues higher education at Redmond College, facing new friendships, romantic interests, and personal growth. This installment delves into Anne's transition from adolescence to adulthood.

Montgomery, L.M. *Anne's House of Dreams.* Boston: L.C. Page & Co., 1917. Anne's life progresses as she marries Gilbert Blythe and they settle into their first home. The novel explores themes of love, loss, and the establishment of a new family.

Montgomery, L.M. *Rainbow Valley.* Boston: L.C. Page & Co., 1919. This installment focuses on Anne's children and their lively interactions with the new minister and his family in the idyllic village of Glen St. Mary.

Montgomery, L.M. *Further Chronicles of Avonlea*. Boston: L.C. Page & Co., 1920. A second collection of short stories set in Avonlea, providing deeper insights into the lives of its residents.

Montgomery, L.M. *Rilla of Ingleside*. Boston: L.C. Page & Co., 1921. The final Anne novel, this book follows Anne's youngest daughter, Rilla, as she comes of age during World War I, portraying the impact of the war on her family and community.

Montgomery, L.M. *Emily of New Moon*. Boston: Frederick A. Stokes Company, 1923. Introducing Emily Starr, a young girl with literary aspirations, this novel parallels Montgomery's own experiences. It offers a deeper exploration of creativity and the struggles of a budding writer.

Montgomery, L.M. *Emily Climbs*. Boston: Frederick A. Stokes Company, 1925. The second book in the Emily series, focusing on Emily's teenage years and her pursuit of writing, despite societal expectations.

Montgomery, L.M. *Emily's Quest*. Boston: Frederick A. Stokes Company, 1927. The final book in the Emily series, exploring Emily's journey to achieve literary success and personal fulfillment.

Montgomery, L.M. *Magic for Marigold*. Boston: Frederick A. Stokes Company, 1929. A standalone novel about Marigold Lesley, a dreamy and imaginative girl growing up in a close-knit family.

Montgomery, L.M. *Pat of Silver Bush*. Boston: Frederick A. Stokes Company, 1933. The story of Pat Gardiner, a girl deeply attached to her family home, Silver Bush, and her love of tradition and stability.

Montgomery, L.M. *Mistress Pat*. Boston: Frederick A. Stokes Company, 1935. A sequel to Pat of Silver Bush, focusing on Pat's later years and her journey through love, loss, and change.

Montgomery, L.M. *Jane of Lantern Hill*. Boston: Frederick A. Stokes Company, 1937. The story of Jane Stuart, a girl who reconnects with her estranged father, discovering a sense of belonging and joy.

Montgomery, L.M. *The Road to Yesterday*. Boston: McClelland and Stewart, 1974 (Posthumous). A collection of short stories set in Anne's world, published long after Montgomery's death.

Montgomery, L.M. *The Blythes Are Quoted*. Boston: Penguin Canada, 2009 (Posthumous). A sequel to Rilla of Ingleside, this book includes short stories and poems interspersed with vignettes of the Blythe family, offering a deeper look at their later years.

Montgomery, L.M. *The Alpine Path:* The Story of My Career. Toronto: Fitzhenry & Whiteside, 1974 (first published in Everywoman's World, 1917). In this autobiographical work, Montgomery reflects on her journey as a writer, offering insights into her personal and professional life. It provides readers with a deeper understanding of her inspirations and challenges.

Montgomery, L.M. *The Complete Journals of L.M. Montgomery: The PEI Years, 1889–1900.* Edited by Mary Henley Rubio and Elizabeth Hillman Waterston. Oxford: Oxford University Press, 2012. This volume presents an unabridged account of Montgomery's early life in Prince Edward Island, offering insights into her formative years, personal experiences, and the environment that influenced her literary creations.

Montgomery, L.M. *The Complete Journals of L.M. Montgomery: The PEI Years, 1901–1911.* Edited by Mary Henley Rubio and Elizabeth Hillman Waterston. Toronto: Oxford University Press, 2013. Continuing from the previous volume, this journal covers Montgomery's early adulthood, including her teaching career, the publication of Anne of Green Gables, and personal milestones, providing a comprehensive view of her life during this period.

Montgomery, L.M. *L.M. Montgomery's Complete Journals: The Ontario Years, 1911–1917.* Edited by Jen Rubio. Oakville: Rock's Hill Press, 2016. This volume details Montgomery's transition to Ontario, her marriage, and the challenges she faced balancing family life with her writing career, offering a candid look into her personal and professional endeavors during these years.

Montgomery, L.M. *L.M. Montgomery's Complete Journals: The Ontario Years, 1918–1921.* Edited by Jen Rubio. Oakville: Rock's Mills Press, 2017.Covering the post-World War I era, this journal reflects on Montgomery's experiences during a time of global change, her family life, and the evolution of her writing career, providing insights into her personal and professional challenges.

Montgomery, L.M. *L.M Montgomery's Complete Journals: The Ontario Years, 1922–1925.* Edited by Jen Rubio. Oakville: Rock's Mills Press, 2018. This edition delves into Montgomery's personal and professional challenges, including her struggles with mental health, family responsibilities, and the pressures of literary fame, offering a deeper understanding of her life during this period.

Montgomery, L.M. *L.M. Montgomery's Complete Journals: The Ontario Years, 1926–1929.* Edited by Jen Rubio. Oakville: Rock's Mills Press, 2017. Focusing on Montgomery's later years in Ontario, this volume discusses her ongoing literary endeavors, personal reflections, and the societal changes of the late 1920s, providing a comprehensive view of her life during these years.

Montgomery, L.M. *L.M. Montgomery's Complete Journals: The Ontario Years, 1930–1933.* Edited by Jen Rubio. Oakville: Rock's Mills Press, 2019. This final volume provides insights into Montgomery's life during the early years of the Great Depression, her reflections on aging, and her enduring commitment to writing despite personal and professional challenges

Montgomery, L.M. *The Watchman and Other Poems.* Boston: L.C. Page & Co., 1916. This collection, the only volume of poetry published during Montgomery's lifetime, comprises 94 poems that explore themes of nature, love, and spirituality. The poems reflect her deep connection to Prince Edward Island and offer insights into the emotional landscape that influenced her prose.

Montgomery, L.M. *The Poetry of Lucy Maud Montgomery.* Selected and introduced by John Ferns and Kevin McCabe. Markham: Fitzhenry & Whiteside, 1987. This posthumous anthology compiles a selection of Montgomery's poetry, aiming to reach readers she considered "kindred spirits." The editors provide an introduction that contextualizes her poetic works within her broader literary career, highlighting her lyrical exploration of nature and human experience.

Montgomery, L.M. *The Green Gables Letters: From L.M. Montgomery to Ephraim Weber, 1905–1909.* Edited by Wilfrid Eggleston. Ottawa: Borealis Press, 1981. This collection comprises letters exchanged between L. M. Montgomery and Ephraim Weber, a fellow writer and correspondent. The letters, written during the years leading up to and following the publication of Anne of Green Gables, provide a candid look into Montgomery's thoughts, challenges, and experiences as she navigated her burgeoning literary career.

Selected Short Stories

Montgomery, L.M. *The Story of Uncle Dick*. New England Magazine, 1897. This early short story highlights Montgomery's flair for storytelling, capturing the quaint charm of small-town life.

Montgomery, L.M. *A Case of Trespass*. Philadelphia Times, 1899. A suspenseful tale showcasing Montgomery's early experimentation with themes of justice and morality.

Montgomery, L.M. *A Strayed Allegiance*. The Housewife, 1900. A story exploring the complexities of loyalty and the unexpected bonds between humans and animals.

Montgomery, L.M. *The Waking of Helen*. Ladies' World, 1901. This tale examines the theme of self-discovery, a precursor to Montgomery's later works on female empowerment.

Montgomery, L.M. *An Unconventional Confidence*. Golden Days for Boys and Girls, 1902. A charming story that celebrates individuality and breaking societal norms.

Montgomery, L.M. *The Red Room*. Sunday Chronicle, 1903. A gothic tale blending suspense and intrigue, reflecting Montgomery's versatility as a storyteller.

Montgomery, L.M. *The Garden of Spices*. Godey's Lady's Book, 1905. A poetic story that captures Montgomery's deep connection to nature and its role in human life.

Montgomery, L.M. *The Strike at Putney*. Munsey's Magazine, 1906. A humorous tale demonstrating Montgomery's knack for weaving wit and satire into her stories.

Montgomery, L.M. *Each in His Own Tongue*. Youth's Companion, 1909. This story reflects on individuality and the universal power of art to connect people.

Selected Poems

Montgomery, L.M. *The Gable Window*. The Boston Evening Transcript, 1895. This poem offers a glimpse into Montgomery's romantic view of everyday life and its quiet beauty.

Montgomery, L.M. *Spring Song*. The Week, 1896. A lyrical ode to the season of renewal, showcasing Montgomery's deep appreciation for nature.

Montgomery, L.M. *When Twilight Falls*. The Canadian Magazine, 1897. A melancholic yet hopeful meditation on endings and beginnings.

Montgomery, L.M. *An Autumn Evening*. Godey's Lady's Book, 1898. A reflective piece capturing the bittersweet beauty of autumn, a recurring theme in Montgomery's work.

Montgomery, L.M. *Down Stream*. The Presbyterian Witness, 1900. This evocative poem explores the flow of time and the unyielding passage of life.

Biographies and Studies of L.M. Montgomery

Rubio, Mary Henley. *Lucy Maud Montgomery: The Gift of Wings*. Toronto: Doubleday Canada, 2008. This comprehensive biography delves into Montgomery's personal and professional life, drawing extensively from her journals and letters. Rubio offers an in-depth exploration of Montgomery's experiences, challenges, and the complexities behind her beloved works.

Gillen, Mollie. *The Wheel of Things: A Biography of L.M. Montgomery*. Don Mills: Fitzhenry & Whiteside, 1975. As one of the earliest modern biographies, Gillen's work provides valuable insights into Montgomery's life and literary career. It explores her personal struggles and the societal context in which she wrote, offering a foundational understanding of her journey.

Epperly, Elizabeth Rollins. *The Fragrance of Sweet-Grass: L.M. Montgomery's Heroines and the Pursuit of Romance*. Toronto: University of Toronto Press, 1992. Epperly examines Montgomery's portrayal of female protagonists and their romantic pursuits. The study analyzes themes of identity, autonomy, and societal expectations, providing a critical perspective on Montgomery's literary contributions.

Reimer, Mavis, ed. Such a *Simple Little Tale: Critical Responses to L.M. Montgomery's Anne of Green Gables*. Metuchen, NJ: Scarecrow Press, 1992. This collection brings together critical essays analyzing "Anne of Green Gables" from various perspectives, including feminist, cultural, and literary view. It offers a comprehensive examination of the novel's themes and its place in literary history.

MacMillan, Don. *Lucy Maud Montgomery: A Writer's Life*. Toronto: Fitzhenry & Whiteside, 1985. Aimed at younger readers, this biography provides an accessible overview of Montgomery's life and achievements, highlighting her journey as a writer and the creation of her famous works.

Bruce, Harry. Maud: *The Life of L.M. Montgomery.* Toronto: Seal Bantam Books, 1992. This biography offers a concise yet insightful exploration of L.M. Montgomery's life, focusing on her formative years and the experiences that shaped her literary career. Drawing from Montgomery's journals and letters, Bruce provides a narrative that highlights her determination to become a writer despite personal and societal challenges. The book delves into her relationships, the creation of Anne of Green Gables, and the impact of her work on Canadian literature.

Prince Edward Island

Green Gables Heritage Place: Cavendish, PE, Canada. The historic farmhouse that inspired "Anne of Green Gables," now a museum offering tours and exhibits.

L.M. Montgomery's Cavendish Home National Historic Site, Cavendish, PE, Canada. The site of Montgomery's family home, featuring the original house's foundation and gardens.

L.M. Montgomery Birthplace, New London, PE, Canada. The house where Montgomery was born, now a museum showcasing her personal artifacts.

Bideford Parsonage Museum, Bideford, PE, Canada. Montgomery lived here during her first teaching position; the museum highlights her early career.

L.M. Montgomery Institute, Charlottetown, PE, Canada. Established in 1993, the Institute promotes research into the life, works, culture, and influence of L.M. Montgomery. It houses a vast collection of her works and related materials.

The College of Piping and Celtic Performing Arts of Canada, Summerside, PE. While not directly related to Montgomery, this institution celebrates the Celtic heritage that influenced much of Prince Edward Island's culture, which is reflected in Montgomery's works.

Ontario

Leaskdale Manse National Historic Site, Uxbridge, ON, Canada. Montgomery's home from 1911 to 1926, where she wrote many of her works; now a museum.

Bala's Museum with Memories of Lucy Maud Montgomery, Bala, ON, Canada. A museum dedicated to Montgomery's visit to Bala in 1922, which inspired her novel "The Blue Castle."

Norval Presbyterian Manse, Norval, ON, Canada. Montgomery's residence from 1926 to 1935; efforts are underway to establish it as a museum. https://lmmontgomerynorval.com/

Heirs of L.M. Montgomery, Toronto, ON, Canada. L.M. Montgomery's literary estate is managed by her descendants, who oversee the rights to her works and ensuretheir proper representation. They collaborate with various organizations to promote Montgomery's legacy and protect the integrity of her publications. https://lmmontgomery.ca/about/permissions

University of Guelph – Archival & Special Collections, Guelph, ON, Canada.The university houses an extensive L.M. Montgomery collection including her personal journals, photographs, and manuscripts, serving as a vital resource for scholars and enthusiasts. https://www.lib.uoguelph.ca/archives/our-collections/m-montgomery/

Authors and Works That Inspired Maud

Alcott, Louisa May. *Little Women.* Boston: Roberts Brothers, 1868. This novel follows the lives of the March sisters as they navigate the challenges of growing up. Alcott's portrayal of strong, independent female characters likely influenced Montgomery's creation of spirited heroines like Anne Shirley.

Austen, Jane. *Emma.* London: John Murray, 1816. Austen's novel centres on Emma Woodhouse, a young woman with a penchant for matchmaking. The intricate social dynamics and character development in Austen's work may have informed Montgomery's own narrative techniques.

Brontë, Charlotte. *Jane Eyre.* London: Smith, Elder & Co., 1847. This Gothic novel tells the story of Jane Eyre, an orphaned girl who becomes a governess and falls in love with her employer. Themes of resilience and self-discovery in Brontë's work resonate with Montgomery's characterizations.

Dickens, Charles. *A Tale of Two Cities.* London: Chapman & Hall, 1859. Set during the French Revolution, this novel explores themes of sacrifice and redemption. Dickens' vivid storytelling and complex characters may have influenced Montgomery's narrative style.

Eliot, George. *Middlemarch.* Edinburgh: William Blackwood and Sons, 1871–72. Eliot's novel examines the lives of residents in a provincial town, delving into social and political issues. The depth of character exploration in Eliot's work likely impacted Montgomery's own character development.

Scott, Sir Walter. *The Lay of the Last Minstrel.* Edinburgh: James Ballantyne, 1805. This narrative poem blends history and romance, reflecting Scott's interest in Scottish folklore. Montgomery's appreciation for folklore and poetic language can be seen as influenced by Scott's works.

Shakespeare, William. *As You Like It.* London: Edward Blount and William Jaggard, 1623. This pastoral comedy explores themes of love and identity. Shakespeare's exploration of human nature and use of wit may have inspired Montgomery's own literary techniques.

Wordsworth, William. *Poems in Two Volumes.* London: Longman, Hurst, Rees, Orme, and Brown, 1807. This collection includes some of Wordsworth's most famous poems, emphasizing nature and emotion. Montgomery's descriptive passages and appreciation for natural beauty reflect Wordsworth's influence.

Additional Sources

Sullivan Entertainment. *Anne of Green Gables: The 1985 Classic Mini-Series.* This television adaptation brought Montgomery's beloved novel to a wider audience, capturing the essence of Anne's character and the charm of Prince Edward Island.

Netflix Series. *Anne with an E.* 2017–2019. A modern re-imagining of Montgomery's classic, this series explores contemporary themes while staying true to the spirit of the original work.

Hanako Muraoka's Japanese translation of Anne of Green Gables, titled *Akage no An,* 1952 by Shinchosha Publishing Co., Ltd. Muraoka's work introduced Anne's story to a post-war Japan, resonating deeply with readers and establishing Anne as a cultural icon. For more details, see Anne's Cradle: The Life of Hanako Muraoka, Translator of Anne of Green Gables by Eri Muraoka.

Author's Biography

Blake, Eric. Photograph of A.C. Blake and Hala, the Studio Cat

A.C. Blake is a Canadian-American poet, author, and illustrator whose works are deeply influenced by her rich heritage and the beauty of natural landscapes. A lifelong admirer of L.M. Montgomery, Blake channels themes of resilience, hope, and human nature in her creative endeavors, weaving together words and images that speak to the heart.

Her poetry, short stories, and illustrations have been published internationally, recognized for their emotional depth and cultural richness. Blake's work has appeared in numerous anthologies and literary journals, with some of her original papers preserved in the prestigious de Grummond Children's Literature Collection at the University of Southern Mississippi.

Blake studied at Emily Carr University in British Columbia and holds an MA from Syracuse University and a terminal MFA from the University of Hartford. She serves as a professor of visual storytelling at Sessions College and continues to explore new ways of blending her love of literature and art in all her projects.

To discover more about her work, visit: annecatharineblake.com.

ALSO BY A.C. BLAKE
(Anne Catharine Blake)

INCLUSION IN POETRY ANTHOLOGIES
Appreciation & Remembering Others

- "Gerald's Flight" — *Remembering Gerald Stern Anthology*
- "In Defiance of the Night" — *Remembering Dylan Thomas*
- "Where Poems May Go: For T.S. Eliot" — *Remembering T.S. Eliot*
- "The Sharp Pain of Freedom" — *Remembering Dennis Brutus*
- "In the Mirror of Sylvia" — *Remembering Sylvia Plath*
- "In the Garden of Audre's Legacy" — *Remembering Audre Lorde*
- "Whispers in the Woods: An Ode to Frost" — *Remembering*
- *Robert Frost*
- "To Walt in the Language of Leaves" — *Walt Whitman, 205*
- "The Invitation" — *Katherine Mansfield KM100 Video*
- "The Heart of Moonstone" — *The Art of Inclusion: The Story of Larry Robin and Moonstone*

Celebrating the World:
United Nations & Global Vision

- "History Has Already Told This Story" — *Poetry Ink Anthology, 29th Annual*
- "Blue Sky and Wheat" — *Support for Ukraine Anthology, 2025*
- "Even Sorrow Floats" — *Haiku Day Anthology, 2025*
- "I Am Article 19" — *World Press Freedom Day Anthology, 2025*
- "Poems Stand Free" — *World Poetry Day Anthology, 2025*
- "What Is Lost in Blindness" — *Human Rights Day Anthology*
- "The Choice Is Ours" — *Chaos! Crisis! Conflict! Anthology*
- "Sonnet to the Muse of Poetry" — *World Poetry Day Anthology, 2024*
- "Barren Sandhill Series" — *Haiku Day Anthology, 2024*
- "Promises to Keep" — *World Environmental Day Anthology, 2024*
- "Freedom's Complications" — *Freedom Anthology, 2024*
- "A Banned Book Speaks" — *Banned Books Anthology, 2024*
- "Circus of Shadows" — *Traitor/Patriot Anthology*

Personal Reflection & Understanding

- "Off Season" — *Bards Across the Pond US/UK*
- "Bright Trails" and "Wisdom" — *Minute Musings*
- "Amethyst's Secret" — *Inheritance: A Poetic Boon by Our Ancestors*
- "Chorus of the Young" and "Canvas of Creation" — *Cadence: Life's Poetic Rhythms*
- "Packing List for Starting Over" — *South Carolina Bards, 2022*
- "Lucky Pennies" — *South Carolina Bards, 2023*
- "Do Little Field" — *South Carolina Bards, 2024*
- "Winter Joy," "Wishing Lights," and "Threads" — *Harmonic Verse*
- "Self-Portrait of a Nomad Compass" — *Poetry Ink Anthology, 28th Annual*
- "Empathy, a Double-Edged Sword" and "Facing My Nemesis, Displaced Loyalty" — *Nemesis: A Stitch in Time Saves Nine*

PRINT AND ONLINE MAGAZINES-POETRY

- "The Problem Is" — *The Listening Eye Literary Magazine, 2024*
- "The Day I Broke Up with Grief" — *Grief Digest Magazine*
- "Peace Bridge Shuffle" — *50word Memoirs*
- "Antarctica Wedding" — *Silk Road Review*
- "The Last Voyageur" (Death Poem) — *WILDsound Writing Festival*
- "The Wooden Witness" (Art Poem) — *WILDsound Writing Festival*
- "Left-Hand Translation" (Life Poem) — *WILDsound Writing Festival*

INCLUSION IN SHORT STORY ANTHOLOGIES

- "The Girl in the Blue Painting" — *BLUE: A Hue Are You*
- "Hala, the Studio Cat" — *Cats Anthology*
- "Mom, Me, and Brian Wilson" — *Thriving: An Anthology*
- "Painting Dreams in Tuscany" — *Lost: Stories of Missing Things*
- "The Culinary Chronicles of Caroline" — *Zinging Success / Comforting Failure*
- "The Rainy-Day Job Interview" — *The Bad Day Book*
- "Dreamscape Delivery" — *Yours Indispensable*
- "Seattle Light" — *Seattle Laughs / Graphic Novel*

AWARD-WINNING CHILDREN'S BOOKS
Illustrated & written by Anne Catharine Blake

- **Sheep Care** – *20th Anniversary Edition (Counting)*
- **Sheep Lost** – *20th Anniversary Edition (Opposites)*
- **Sheep Share** – *20th Anniversary Edition (Emotions)*
- **Sheep Sleep** – *20th Anniversary Edition (Colors)*

Thank you for reading.

*If Celebrating Maud touched your heart,
please consider leaving a kind review
or sharing it with someone who might enjoy it, too.*

With gratitude,
A.C. Blake
annecatharineblake.com

www.ingramcontent.com/pod-product-compliance
Lightning Source LLC
Chambersburg PA
CBHW040640100526
44585CB00039B/2878